AF526754

SCIENCE EXPERIMENTS

Chemical Reactions

Om SPARKS

An Imprint of Om Books International

Om SPARKS An Imprint of Om Books International

Reprinted in 2026

Corporate & Editorial Office
A-12, Sector 64, Noida 201 301
Uttar Pradesh, India
Phone: +91 120 477 4100
Email: editorial@ombooks.com
Website: www.ombooksinternational.com

Sales Office
107, Ansari Road, Darya Ganj
New Delhi 110 002, India
Phone: +91 11 4000 9000
Email: sales@ombooks.com
Website: www.ombooks.com

ISBN: 978-93-52763-07-8

Printed in India

10 9 8 7 6 5 4 3

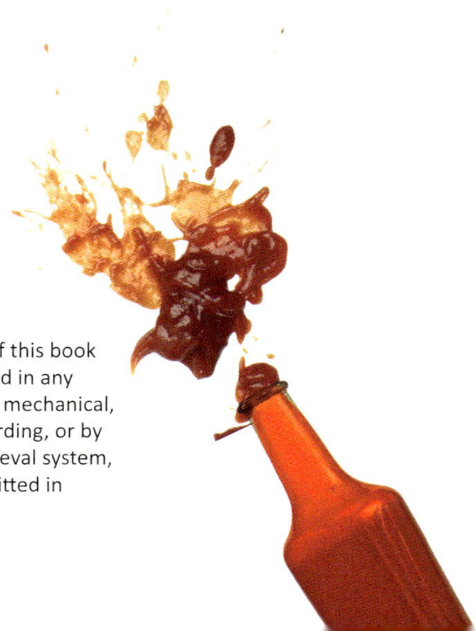

CONTENTS

Duration of Experiment

This icon indicates approximately how long the experiment will take, including the set-up time.

Difficulty Level

The black bars in this icon indicate level of difficulty in doing this experiment with one icon depicting the least level of difficulty.

Adult Supervision

This icon indicates that parental supervision is required. Always have an adult beside you.

NOTE: All activities and experiments described in this book should be ideally performed with adult supervision. Parents anc guardians are advised to oversee the children and assist them with any difficult or potentially harmful tools. Common sense and discretion are advised. The publisher does not assume any responsibility for any injuries or damages arising from any activities.

Tsp - teaspoon Tbsp - tablespoon ml - millilitre l - litre gm - gram 1 cup - 250 millilitre cm - centimetre

Smoking Hot

Duration of Experiment: 1 hour

Difficulty Level:

What you need:

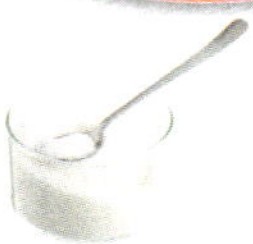
1 cup sugar

3 cups potassium nitrate

Pan

Aluminium foil

5 cm string

Lighter

Naphtha lighter fluid

What to do:

Step 1. Dip the string in the lighter fluid. Let it dry.

Step 2. Pour potassium nitrate and sugar into the pan. Heat it on a low flame.

Step 3. Use long strokes to stir the mixture till it is nearly liquid.

Step 4. Once it is brown, take it off the heat.

Step 5. Empty it into an aluminium foil. This is now your smoke bomb.

Step 6. Put the dry string in the smoke bomb.

Step 7. Allow the bomb to cool and peel off the aluminium foil. Light it and stand back.

Perform this experiment only in an open area and under strict adult supervision.

What just happened?

When heated, the sugar and potassium nitrate react and form a substance called potassium carbonate. This solid is dispersed into the air blocking light, thus giving the 'smoky' effect.

Bubbly Colours

Duration of Experiment: 10 mins.

Difficulty Level:

What you need:

Food colour

Paint palette

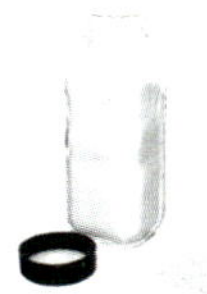
4 tsp baking soda

2 tbsp cooking vinegar

What to do:

Step 1. Fill four sections of the palette with cooking vinegar.

Step 2. Put a drop of each colour in different sections.

Step 3. Put a teaspoon of baking soda into each section.

Step 4. Watch your colours fizz!

What just happened? The cooking vinegar and baking soda react to form carbon dioxide, which causes all the fizzy bubbles.

Potato Starch

Duration of Experiment: 10 mins.

Difficulty Level:

What you need:

Potato

Iodine solution

Plate

Water

What to do:

Step 1. Boil and mash the potato.

Step 2. Put this on a plate and put two drops of iodine on the potato.

Step 3. Watch the iodine solution change from a brown, to a purple blue colour.

What just happened? Potato contains a certain chemical called 'starch'. When this starch is in the presence of iodine, it turns blue.

Invisible Ink

Duration of Experiment: 20 mins.

Difficulty Level:

What you need:

Bowl

Ear bud

½ lemon

White paper

Iron

Water

What to do:

Step 1. Squeeze the lemon into the bowl.
Add a few drops of water to it.
Step 2. Mix the water and lemon juice.
Step 3. Dip one end of your ear bud into the solution.
Step 4. Write a message on the white paper.
Step 5. To read the secret message, run a hot iron over it.

What just happened?

Lemon juice oxidises and turns brown when heated. Diluting it makes it hard to notice till it is heated!

Glowing Goo

Duration of Experiment: 5 mins.

Difficulty Level:

What you need:

1 tsp borax

½ cup glue

Bowl and Whisk

1½ cup warm water

½ tbsp glow in the dark paint

What to do:

Step 1. Mix the borax with 1 cup of warm water.
Step 2. Add the paint to this mixture.
Step 3. Separately whisk the glue and the remaining water with a whisk.
Step 4. Mix both solutions with your hand.
Step 5. Drain out the extra water. Enjoy the glowing goo.

What just happened?

When the glue and the borax are combined in a water solution, they react and create one giant molecule that can absorb large amounts of water. This glows in the dark when you mix the paint with it.

Hot Soap

Duration of Experiment: 5 mins.

Difficulty Level:

What you need:

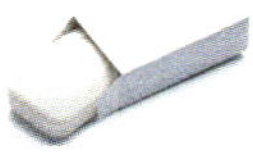

Soap bar

Flat microwave dish

Microwave

What to do:

Step 1. Put the soap on the microwave dish.

Step 2. Microwave it for two minutes.

Step 3. Watch the phenomenal growth of your soap!

! Don't leave the microwave and soap unattended.

What just happened?

When you heat the soap, you not only soften it but also heat the air and water trapped inside it. The water vaporises and the air expands. The expanding gases push on the soft soap, creating the foam.

Colour Changing Juice

Duration of Experiment: 5 mins.

Difficulty Level:

What you need:

5 lemons

2 tsp baking soda

Grape juice

Glasses

What to do:

Step 1. Empty the grape juice into one glass.

Step 2. Squeeze the lemons into this glass.

Notice the colour change from purple to pink!

Step 3. In the other glass, mix some grape juice and baking soda. Watch the colour change from purple to green!

What just happened?

Grape juice indicates whether a substance is acidic or basic. Therefore, the acidic lemon causes it to change colour, as does the baking soda.

Coloured Chemicals

Duration of Experiment: 25 mins.

Difficulty Level:

What you need:

2 lemons

Knife

Sieve

½ red cabbage

2 tbsp baking soda

Bowls

Water

What to do:

Step 1. Chop the red cabbage and bring it to a boil on the stove with the help of an adult.

Step 2. Let it soak for 15 minutes. Stir it occasionally.

Step 3. Once cool, strain the water and discard the cabbage.

Step 4. Squeeze the lemons and mix the juice with the strained cabbage water in one bowl.

Step 5. Mix baking soda with the strained water in another bowl.

Step 6. Now mix these two solutions in a third bowl.

Step 7. Watch as the pink and green solutions mix and turn purple!

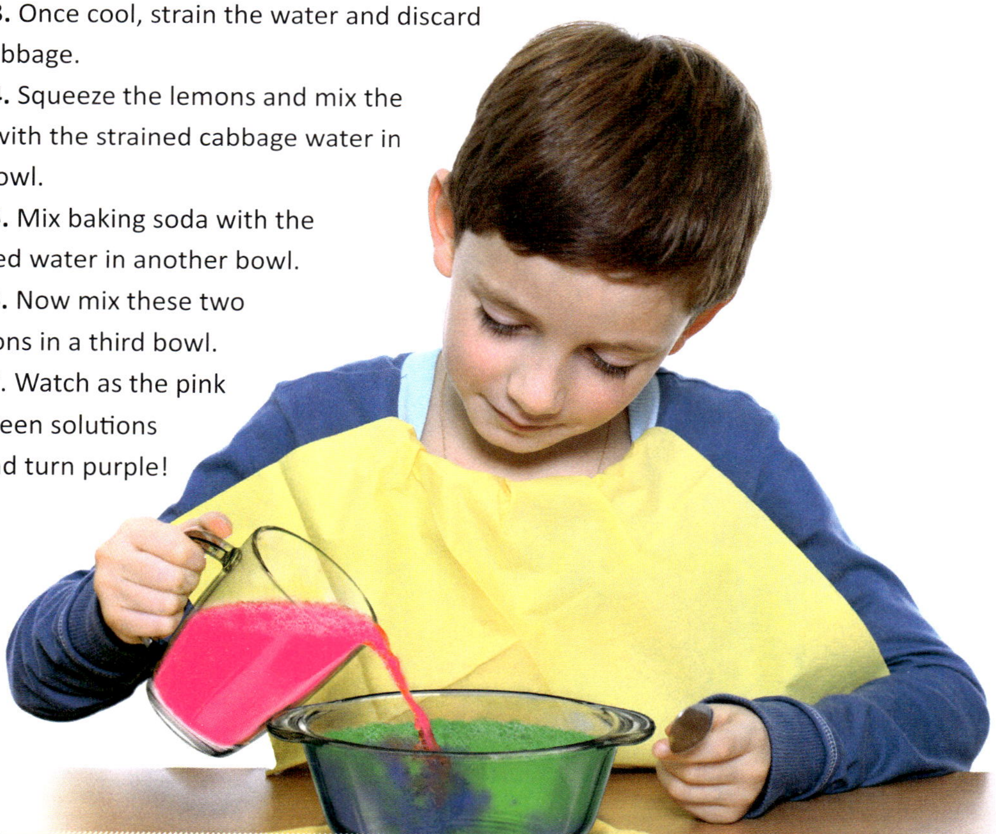

What just happened?

When citric acid and baking soda are mixed, they neutralise the reactions that took place. The pink solution and green solution mix to form a third purple solution.

Smoky Snake

Duration of Experiment: 10 mins.

Difficulty Level:

What you need:

Protective eyewear and gloves

10 gm sugar

100 ml sulphuric acid

Strong glass

! This reaction creates a lot of heat, so be careful while handling the glass.

What to do:

Step 1. Wear protective eyewear and gloves.

Step 2. Put the sugar in a strong glass.

Step 3. Add the sulphuric acid to the glass and stir well.

Step 4. Wait for around 10 minutes and watch a smoky snake rise out of the glass!

What just happened?

The water from the sugar got sucked up by the acid and formed carbon. This carbon, along with water vapour, is what you saw as the snake.

Blood Explosions

Duration of Experiment: 10 mins.

Difficulty Level:

What you need:

3 tbsp baking soda

Ketchup

Bottle

Water

What to do:

Step 1. Mix a little water and some ketchup in the bottle.

Step 2. Add the baking soda to the ketchup.

Step 3. Shut the lid of the bottle and shake it.

Step 4. Put it down and wait for the explosion.

! This experiment is quite messy, so make sure you do it in the kitchen or some place that's easy to clean up.

What just happened?

The ketchup contains acid, which reacts with the baking soda to create carbon dioxide. The gas bubbles rose up through the ketchup resulting in the explosion.

Vanishing Water

Duration of Experiment: 10 mins.

Difficulty Level:

What you need:

1 tbsp sodium polyacrylate (available in lab supply stores and online)

Water

Opaque mug

What to do:

Step 1. Challenge a friend that you can make water disappear.

Step 2. Before you begin, put the sodium polyacrylate in the mug.

Step 3. Show your friend that you are pouring water into the mug.

Step 4. In a few minutes, turn the cup over. Nothing pours out!

What just happened?

The polyacrylate absorbs the water and turns into a gel. Polyacrylate has the ability to absorb as much as 200 to 300 times its mass in water.

Green Ball

Duration of Experiment: 10 mins.

Difficulty Level:

What you need:

Styrofoam beads

Glue

Green food colour

Ziplock bag

1 tbsp borax

1 cup water

What to do:

Step 1. Mix borax in half a cup of water.

Step 2. Mix glue and ¼th cup water. Add the food colour.

Step 3. Pour both solutions into the ziplock bag. Don't mix it.

Step 4. Add the styrofoam beads.

Step 5. Seal the bag and knead it with your hand till it is mixed.

Step 6. Take it out and shape it as you wish.

What just happened?

When the glue and the borax are combined in a water solution, they create one giant molecule. The styrofoam beads help keep the shape.

Create Oxygen

Duration of Experiment: 20 mins.

Difficulty Level:

What you need:

2 tbsp yeast

Toothpicks

Small glass jar with lid

Burning candle

100 ml hydrogen peroxide (3%)

What to do:

Step 1. Pour the hydrogen peroxide into the jar.

Step 2. Add the yeast to the jar. Cover it.

Step 3. Once bubbles begin to form, light a toothpick and extinguish it.

Step 4. While the toothpick is still glowing, remove the lid and insert the toothpick in the neck of the jar.

Step 5. Your flame will be revived.

! Always be careful when handling fire. Never use fire in the absence of an adult.

What just happened?

The reaction between the yeast and the hydrogen peroxide created oxygen. Fire needs oxygen to burn. So, when you put the smouldering toothpick into the jar, the oxygen revived the flame.

Sticking Together

Duration of Experiment: 15 mins.

Difficulty Level:

What you need:

Brush

Spoon

1 cup flour

½ cup water

Jar

Newspaper

What to do:

Step 1. Mix the flour and water in the jar.

Step 2. Stir the mixture well for five minutes.

Step 3. Spread the glue on the newspaper with the brush and let it dry for 15 minutes.

What just happened?

A chemical reaction took place once the flour was mixed with the water. The water evaporated and the flour held the paper together.

Gelatine Mobile

Duration of Experiment: 48 hours.

Difficulty Level: ◇ ◇ ◇

What you need:

Plastic lid

Cookie cutters

Food colour

3 small packets gelatine

Saucepan

Straw

Wooden spoon

5 tbsp water

What to do:

Step 1. Cook water, food colouring and gelatine in a saucepan on a low heat on the stove till it is thick.

Step 2. Pour the liquid into the plastic lid and remove the bubbles with the spoon.

Step 3. Let the mixture cool for 45 minutes.

Step 4. Carefully take the gelatine out of the plastic lid.

Step 5. While the gelatine is still elastic, use the cookie cutters to cut out various shapes.

Step 6. Use the straw to make holes in the shapes, so they can be hung.

Step 7. Leave them out to dry for a couple of days and they'll be as hard as plastic!

What just happened?

Gelatine dissolves in water only when heated, but not when it is cool. So when the gelatine solution cooled down, it formed a semi-solid mass or gel.

Jumping Spaghetti

Duration of Experiment: 20 mins.

Difficulty Level:

What you need:

2 tbsp baking soda

Glass

1 cup cooking vinegar

Water

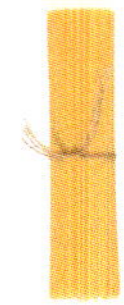

Strands of uncooked spaghetti

What to do:

Step 1. Dissolve the baking soda in the glass of water. Add cooking vinegar.

Step 2. Break the spaghetti into one-inch pieces. Put 6 of these in the glass.

Step 3. Watch your spaghetti jump up and down in the glass.

What just happened?

The reaction between vinegar and baking soda created carbon dioxide. This gas sticks to the spaghetti and makes it float on water. Hence, it rises up. On reaching the surface, the gas is released into the air and the spaghetti sinks down again.

Speedy Rust

Duration of Experiment: 2 hours.

Difficulty Level:

What you need:

Steel wool

Glass

Gloves

3 tbsp bleach

Water

3 tbsp cooking vinegar

What to do:

Step 1. Put the steel wool in the glass.

Step 2. Fill the glass with water.

Step 3. Pour in the cooking vinegar and bleach.

Step 4. Wait for two hours and see your steel wool pad rust!

What just happened?

Rust forms when iron is combined with moisture and oxygen. The oxygen in the bleach combines with the iron in the wool to form rust.

Rainbow in a Glass

Duration of Experiment: 30 mins.

Difficulty Level:

What you need:

Honey

Dishwashing liquid

Water

Vegetable oil

Rubbing alcohol

Tall glass

Blue food colouring

What to do:

Step 1. Fill ¼th of the glass with honey.

Step 2. Tip the glass slightly and add the dishwashing liquid.

Step 3. Mix some food colouring and water, and add it to the glass.

Step 4. Add some vegetable oil to the mixture.

Step 5. Finally, add the rubbing alcohol and see the rainbow colours.

What just happened? Denser liquids settle at the bottom, while the less dense liquids float to the top.

Sparkly Explosion

Duration of Experiment: 10 mins.

Difficulty Level:

What you need:

Tray

2 tsp blue glitter

2 tbsp baking soda

5 drops of red food colour

Vase

½ cup cooking vinegar

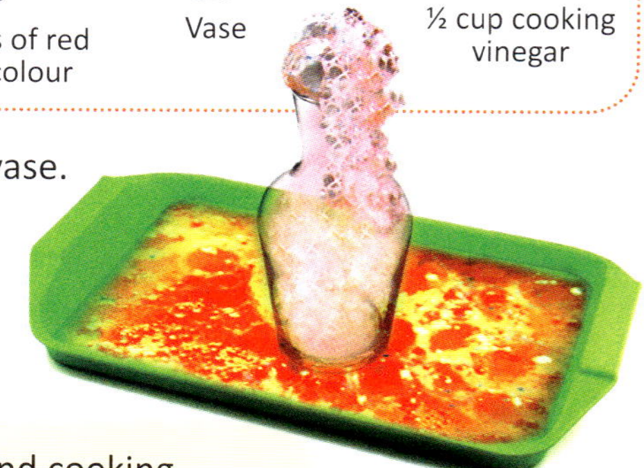

What to do:

Step 1. Put the baking soda in the vase.

Step 2. Place this vase on the tray.

Step 3. Add the food colour and glitter.

Step 4. Pour in the cooking vinegar quickly.

Step 5. Enjoy your shiny display.

What just happened? The baking soda and cooking vinegar react to form carbonic acid, which is an unstable substance. It breaks apart into water and carbon dioxide, creating all the fizz.

Hot Ice cream

Duration of Experiment: 1 hour

Difficulty Level:

What you need:

3 eggs

¼ tsp cream of tartar

¼ tsp salt

½ tsp vanilla essence

1 cup sugar

Cookies

Ice cream

Baking tray

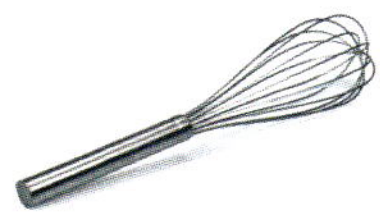
Egg whisk

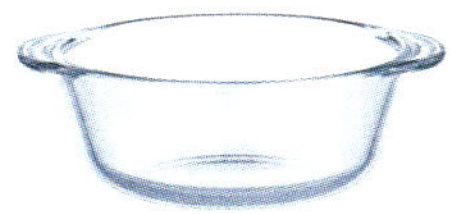
Bowl

Oven

What to do:

Step 1. Separate the egg whites from the yolks in the bowl.

Step 2. Add the cream of tartar, salt and vanilla essence to the egg whites.

Step 3. Whip the whites till they are nice and fluffy.

Step 4. Add sugar by sprinkling 1 tbsp at a time over the mixture.

Step 5. Keep stirring the mixture.

Step 6. Put the cookies in the baking tray at an equal distance from each other.

Step 7. Now put a small scoop of ice cream on each of the cookies.

Step 8. Coat the ice cream with the mixture you just prepared.

Step 9. Bake your ice cream cookie in an oven at 110°C.

Step 10. Take it out after an hour and enjoy your piping hot ice cream!

What just happened?

Cream of tartar is acidic. When it turns moist, it releases carbon dioxide. There are air pockets in the whipped egg, too. The sugar in the mixture hardens when heated and traps the air in the mixture. Air is a poor conductor of heat and therefore protects the ice cream from the heat of the oven.

Volcano Vesuvius

Duration of Experiment: 15 mins.

Difficulty Level:

What you need:

2 tsp baking soda

Clay

Plastic bottle

½ cup cooking vinegar

5 drops red food colour

Container

What to do:

Step 1. Pat some clay around the plastic bottle in the shape of a volcano. You can paint it brown and paint some trees on it to make it look more realistic.

Step 2. Put the baking soda in the bottle.

Step 3. Separately, pour the cooking vinegar into the container till it is half full. Mix the food colour with this.

Step 4. Then, pour this mixture into the bottle. Watch as your volcano erupts in your room!

What just happened?

The baking soda and cooking vinegar react to form carbonic acid, which is an unstable substance. It breaks apart into water and carbon dioxide, creating all the fizz.

SCIENCE AROUND US

Why do volcanoes erupt?

The layer just below the surface of the Earth is known as the 'mantle'. Sometimes, certain conditions cause the mantle to get heated and become liquid. When the pressure is high enough, this liquid searches for weak spots on the Earth's surface and shoots out in the form of red, hot lava.

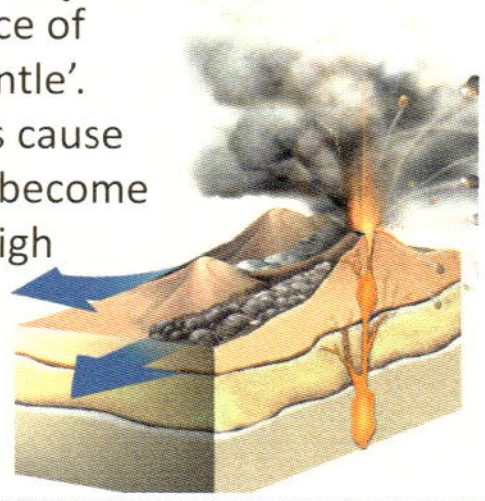

Stink it Up

Duration of Experiment: 4 days

Difficulty Level:

What you need:

Scissors

Jar

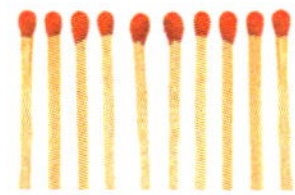

20 strike-any-where match-sticks

2 tbsp household ammonia (available at grocery stores and supermarkets)

What to do:

Step 1. Cut the heads of the matchsticks.

Step 2. Put them in the jar and add the ammonia.

Step 3. Close the jar and swirl the contents around.

Step 4. Wait for 4 days and then open the jar to unleash the stench!

! The fumes from hydrogen sulphide are flammable and can be toxic. Make sure you perform the experiment in a well–ventilated place and be careful.

What just happened?

The matchstick heads are made out of phosphorus sulphide. The phosphorus sulphide and ammonia react to form a nasty smelling substance called ammonium sulphide.

Changing Colours

Duration of Experiment: 20 mins.

Difficulty Level:

What you need:

Knife | Sieve | 1 lemon | ½ red cabbage | Container | Water

What to do:

Step 1. Chop the red cabbage and bring it to boil on the stove.

Step 2. Stir well and leave it to soak for about 15 minutes.

Step 3. Once cool, drain the water and throw the cabbage away.

Step 4. Put the cabbage water in the container. Squeeze the lemon.

Step 5. Notice the colour change.

What just happened?

A chemical in the red cabbage reacts with the citric acid in the lemon and turns pink.

Dancing Mothballs

Duration of Experiment: 15 mins.

Difficulty Level:

What you need:

4 mothballs | Glass | 2 tsp baking soda | ½ cup cooking vinegar | Water

What to do:

Step 1. Dissolve the baking soda in a glass of water.

Step 2. Add the cooking vinegar.

Step 3. Put the mothballs in the glass.

Step 4. Watch the mothballs rise to the surface and sink down again.

What just happened?

The reaction between cooking vinegar and baking soda created carbon dioxide gas. This gas stuck to the mothballs and made them float on the water. The gas was released into the air, and the mothballs sank down again.

Crazy Putty

Duration of Experiment: 12 mins.

Difficulty Level:

What you need:

Container

Glue

1 tbsp borax

Spoon

Water

What to do:

Step 1. Fill the bottom of the container with glue.

Step 2. Add the same amount of water and stir.

Step 3. Add borax. Stir the mixture.

Step 4. It will soon join together, acting like putty!

What just happened? When the glue and the borax are combined in a water solution, they react. This creates one giant molecule. The new compound can absorb large amounts of water, producing a putty-like substance that you can squish in your hands or even bounce.

Bag Bomb

Duration of Experiment: 10 mins.

Difficulty Level:

What you need:

Ziplock bag

3 tsp baking soda

¼ cup warm water

½ cup cooking vinegar

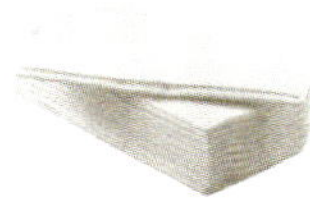

Tissue paper

! Don't stand too close to the bag.

What to do:

Step 1. Pour the warm water in the ziplock bag. Add the cooking vinegar.

Step 2. Wrap the baking soda in the tissue paper.

Step 3. Close half the ziplock bag. Through the open half, put the tissue paper in the bag and close it.

Step 4. Put the bag in the sink. Step back. The bag will begin to expand, and finally burst with a bang!

What just happened?

The baking soda and cooking vinegar create a reaction, which releases carbon dioxide. The carbon dioxide fills the bag till the bag can no longer hold it and it bursts.

Good Juice, Bad Juice

Duration of Experiment: 30 mins.

Difficulty Level:

What you need:

Glasses

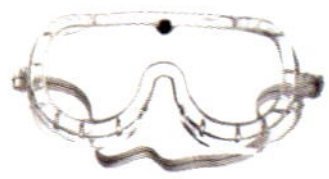

Safety goggles

Rubber gloves

½ tsp cooking vinegar

Water

What to do:

Step 1. Wear the safety goggles and rubber gloves.

Step 2. In the first glass, add water and grape juice.

Step 3. In the second, add ammonia.

Step 4. In the third, add vinegar.

Step 5. Gather an audience.

Step 6. Start off with the first glass, saying that it is good juice.

Step 7. Pour it into the second glass. The juice will turn green. Say that the good juice has now turned bad.

Step 8. Finally, ask the audience to pray real hard for the juice to turn good again.

Step 9. Pour this solution into the last glass, and voila! The liquid returns to its original colour.

! **Do not** try to drink ANY of the solutions created during this experiment. Use gloves while conducting the experiment, as ammonia can cause tissue damage if it comes in contact with your skin.

What just happened?

When you poured the grape juice into the ammonia, it created an alkaline solution which was green in colour. In the third glass, the acidic vinegar neutralises the alkaline solution, returning it to its original colour.

Bag Blast

Duration of Experiment: 10 mins.

Difficulty Level:

What you need:

6 lemons

1 tsp baking soda

50ml Water

Ziplock bag

Don't stand too close to the bag.

What to do:

Step 1. Squeeze the lemons into the ziplock bag.

Step 2. Add baking soda with the spoon.

Step 3. Quickly add water and shut it.

Step 4. Put it in the sink and leave it.

Step 5. The bag becomes extremely cold and blows up!

What just happened?

Lemon contains citric acid. This acid reacts with the water and baking soda. The reaction creates carbon dioxide, which fills the bag and causes it to blow up.

Colour Symphony

Duration of Experiment: 5 mins.

Difficulty Level:

What you need:

Food colour

Tray

Whole milk

5 drops of dishwashing soap

What to do:

Step 1. Pour a thin layer of milk onto the tray.

Step 2. Add six drops of different coloured food colour onto the milk in different spots.

Step 3. Add the dishwashing soap onto the drops of food colour.

Step 4. Watch the colours go beserk.

What just happened?

Soap breaks down fat. The liquid soap onto the tray tried to break down the fat in the milk. While it was doing that, it caused the colours to scatter.

Bottled Cannon

Duration of Experiment: 10 mins.

Difficulty Level:

What you need:

Cork

1 tsp baking soda

4 tbsp cooking vinegar

2 pencils

Tissue paper

Wine bottle

What to do:

! Make sure no one is in the path of the cork.

Step 1. Put the cooking vinegar in the bottle. It should not spill over when the bottle is laid on its side.

Step 2. Wrap the baking soda in the tissue paper. Put it in the bottle.

Step 3. Quickly cork the bottle.

Step 4. Lay the bottle across two horizontal pencils.

Step 5. Wait for the cork to fly off!

What just happened?

The pressure produced by the generated carbon dioxide caused the cork to blow out and the bottle to recoil.

Mould it

Duration of Experiment: 10 mins.

Difficulty Level:

What you need:

Oranges

Cotton balls

Ziplock bag

Rubber gloves

! Handle the mouldy oranges with gloves. Don't eat or smell the mould.

What to do:

Step 1. Leave the oranges in the open for a day.

Step 2. Place them with a damp cotton ball in the ziplock bag.

Step 3. Seal it and put it in a warm, damp place.

Step 4. Check the bag after two weeks.

Step 5. You will see little fuzzy balls on the oranges.

What just happened?

The little fuzzy balls are called 'mould'. It is a form of fungus that grows faster in warm, moist places.

Ready to Launch

Duration of Experiment: 5 mins.

Difficulty Level:

What you need:

35 mm film canister

1 antacid tablet

Tray

3 tbsp water

What to do:

Step 1. Find a large, open space.

Step 2. Remove the lid of the canister and put the water in it.

Step 3. Quickly put the tablet in the canister and seal it tight with the lid.

Step 4. Immediately put the canister down, with the lid on the tray.

Step 5. After about 10 seconds, the film canister will launch into the air.

Stay far away from the rocket.

What just happened?

The water and antacid reacted to form carbon dioxide. This increased the pressure in the canister. The pressure built up till the rocket blasted. This system of thrust is how a real rocket works, whether it is in outer space or here in the Earth's atmosphere.

Tsunami

Duration of Experiment: 10 mins.

Difficulty Level:

What you need:

35 mm film canister

Clay

1 antacid tablet

Bucket

Water

What to do:

Step 1. Fill the bucket with water.

Step 2. Coat the canister with the clay so that it looks like a volcano. It should also be heavy enough to keep the canister from floating.

Step 3. Fill $\frac{1}{3}^{rd}$ of the canister with water.

Step 4. Break the Antacid tablet and drop one quarter into the canister.

Step 5. Close the canister and stick it at the bottom of the bucket which is filled with water.

Step 6. After a minute, the canister lid will fly off, causing a tsunami-like wave.

What just happened?

The reaction in the canister produces carbon dioxide. The carbon dioxide increases the pressure, till the force is enough to force open the lid of the canister. The disturbance underwater pushes a relatively large volume of water to the surface, creating a model tsunami.

Make Slime

Duration of Experiment: 5 mins.

Difficulty Level:

What you need:

Bowl

¼ cup liquid starch

6 drops of food colour

¼ cup water

Spoon

¼ cup glue

What to do:

Step 1. Pour all the water into the bowl.

Step 2. Add the glue and mix well.

Step 3. Add food colour to the mixture.

Step 4. Now add the liquid starch and stir it in.

Step 5. You just made fake slime!

What just happened?

Glue is made up of tiny strands. The liquid starch helps these strands to stay together, giving it a slimy feel.

Fishing Ice

Duration of Experiment: 15 mins.

Difficulty Level:

What you need:

Salt

String

Ice cubes

Glass

What to do:

Step 1. Put an ice cube in a glass.

Step 2. Dangle the string and hold it still over the ice cube.

Step 3. Sprinkle some salt on it.

Step 4. Wait for two minutes and lift your ice cube with the string.

What just happened?

Salt lowers the freezing point of water. The salt begins to crystallise and ice refreezes around the string. This makes the ice cube stick to the string.

Green Coins

Duration of Experiment: 24 hours.

Difficulty Level:

What you need:

Tissue paper

Plate

1 tbsp salt

Copper coins

Bowl

3 tbsp cooking vinegar

What to do:

Step 1. Fold the tissue paper so that it is thick.

Step 2. Mix the salt and cooking vinegar in the bowl.

Soak the tissue in this mixture.

Step 3. Lay the tissue on the plate.

Step 4. Wrap the coins in the tissue.

Step 5. Check the coins the next day. They should have turned green!

What just happened? The copper reacts with carbon dioxide in the air to form copper carbonate, which is green in colour. This reaction usually takes a long time to take place. The cooking vinegar and salt speeds up this reaction.

Make Fake Snot

Duration of Experiment: 5 mins.

Difficulty Level:

What you need:

Fork | Cup | Gelatine | ¼ cup corn syrup | Green food colouring | Boiling water

What to do:

Step 1. Fill half a cup with boiling water.
Step 2. Add 3 tsp of gelatine powder to it. Let it soften before stirring with a fork.
Step 3. Add the corn syrup and green food colouring.
Step 4. Stir it again. It looks like snot, doesn't it?

What just happened?

Mucus is made mostly of sugars and protein. This is exactly what you used to make the fake snot. The long, fine strings you see inside the fake snot when you moved it around are protein strands.

Kitchen Indication

Duration of Experiment: 25 mins.

Difficulty Level:

What you need:

½ red cabbage | Container | Water | Sieve | 1 tbsp baking soda | Knife | Glass

What to do:

Step 1. Chop the red cabbage and boil it in water on the stove.
Step 2. Stir well and leave it to soak for about 15 minutes.
Step 3. Once cool, strain the now purple cabbage water and discard the cabbage.
Step 4. Put the cabbage water in the container. Add the baking soda.
Step 5. Notice the colour change.

What just happened?

A chemical in the red cabbage reacts with the baking soda and turns green.

Rusty

Duration of Experiment: 48 hours.

Difficulty Level:

What you need:

Test tube

Container

2 tsp cooking vinegar

Water

Steel wool

What to do:

Step 1. Dip the steel wool in a mixture of vinegar and water.

Step 2. Put some steel wool in the test tube.

Step 3. Fill the container with water.

Step 4. Invert the test tube and place it in the container.

Step 5. Leave your apparatus untouched for two days.

You will see the steel wool rust and the water level in the test tube rise.

SCIENCE AROUND US

Why do objects rust?

Rust is the common name for a compound called iron oxide (Fe_2O_3). Iron (Fe) combines with oxygen from the air very easily. Actually, iron reacts with oxygen so easily that pure iron is rarely found in nature. When iron (or steel) reacts with oxygen, it forms the red coloured substance called iron oxide.

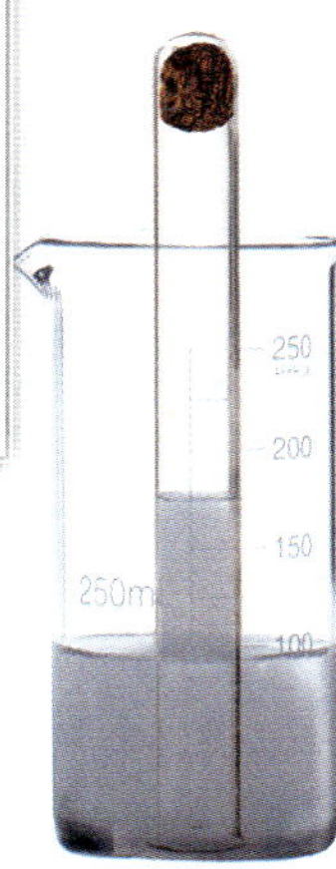

What just happened?

The vinegar helped speed up the process of rusting. This used up the oxygen. As the oxygen in the air was being used up, the air pressure decreased and the water was sucked into the tube.

Strawberry DNA

Duration of Experiment: 1 hour.

Difficulty Level:

What you need:

Strawberry

¼ tsp salt

Ziplock bag

Dishwashing liquid

5 ml isopropyl alcohol (available at a chemist store)

What to do:

Step 1. Put the isopropyl alcohol in the freezer.
Step 2. Mix the water, dishwashing liquid and salt in the plastic container.
Step 3. Put a strawberry in the ziplock bag. Remove as much air as you can, to flatten it.
Step 4. Smash the strawberry with your hands till there are no chunks left.
Step 5. Pour this pulp and the solution you made earlier into another container through the sieve.
Step 6. Separate around 50 - 100 ml of this solution and add the isopropyl alcohol to it.
Step 7. The white layer on top of the rest of the solution is the DNA of the strawberry.
Step 8. You can remove this using tweezers.

What just happened?

All living things contain DNA. The solution you made with the dishwashing liquid and the salt acts as an extraction solution. The soap dissolves the cell membranes. The salt breaks up protein chains that hold nucleic acid together. Finally, DNA is not soluble in isopropyl alcohol, making it easy to identify.

Milk Plastic!

Duration of Experiment: 2 days.

Difficulty Level:

What you need:

Strainer

Cutters

1 tbsp cooking vinegar

Cup

Warm milk

What to do:

Step 1. Put a tablespoon of cooking vinegar in a cup of warm milk and stir it well.
Step 2. Pour the milk through the strainer. You should be left with a white lumpy solid.
Step 3. Wait for it to cool. Cut it with a cutter or press it into any shape you like and let it dry for a few days.

Don't try to drink the milk or eat the plastic!

What just happened?

You made a protein called 'casein'. This protein in the milk reacted with the acid in the vinegar and formed lumps, which were easy to mould.

Chemical Garden

Duration of Experiment: 2 hours.

Difficulty Level:

What you need:

Water glass

Metal salt crystals

Jam jar

Water

What to do:

Step 1. Fill $\frac{1}{3}$rd of the jar with water glass.

Step 2. Fill the rest with water.

Step 3. Drop in some metal salt crystals (such as copper sulphate, lead nitrate, aluminium sulphate, ferrous chloride, etc.).

Step 4. Place your jar on a still surface.

Step 5. In a few hours, you will see your crystals 'growing'.

Step 6. Once you are happy with your garden, replace the solution with water.

! Be careful that the crystals don't break when you pour out the water glass.

What just happened?

The metal salts react with the water glass to form the beautifully coloured precipitant.

OTHER TITLES IN THIS SERIES

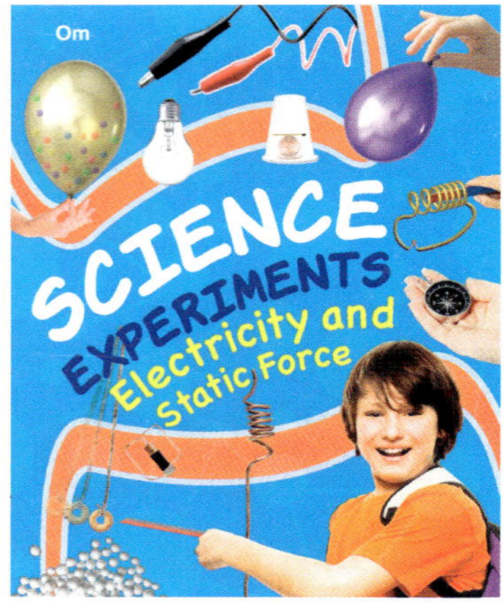